The 10 Quickest Ways to Improve Your Game

By Ian Clark *with* Leo Luongo

Printed in the United States of America

ISBN 1-449-56292-2
EAN-13 978-1-449-56292-2

Credits:
Cover and book design by Rob Hicks
Photography by Jeff Vinnick, courtesy of Vancouver Canucks®

CONTENTS

PREFACE

By Roberto Luongo

Since breaking into the NHL, I have had the opportunity to be coached by Ian Clark for over half of my career. During this time, he has uncovered countless details that help me to improve my game. Indeed, the very improvements that he, and my brother Leo, write about in this handbook are mechanics, tools and philosophies that I use daily to drive my game forward.

I was introduced to Ian in 2001 when he joined the Florida Panthers' coaching staff. He and I stayed in close contact after he left Florida for Vancouver the very next season. Ironically, when my time ended in Florida with my trade to Vancouver, he and I were reunited. Small adjustments in my stance and depth positioning have allowed me to climb out of funks while innovative approaches and tactics that he brings each year help me to continue to push my game forward.

Ian provides support in all aspects of my game. From technical and tactical expertise to mental challenges that confront us all as the season unfolds. He is an invaluable resource as a coach, friend and mentor.

In the summers I spend some of my summer training with my brother Leo. He helped me get ready for the Canadian Olympic Team Orientation Camp. His growth and maturation as a goaltending coach was never more evident than during this preparation period. While he always had a feel for the position and the game, he was able to play a critical role in my summer preparations.

I would strongly recommend "The 10 Quickest Ways to Improve Your Game" to every goaltender, at every level of play, as it will help you, as it helps me, stop more pucks and allow my team to be more competitive. Sometimes the most powerful concepts are the easiest to implement. This handbook is an easy read and highlights simple improvements that you, yourself, can add to your game. It is an excellent resource for committed goalies, parents and coaches.

Good luck with your goaltending,

Roberto Luongo

INTRODUCTION

First and foremost this handbook is NOT meant to be a technical book on goaltending. Instead, the focus of this handbook is to provide goaltenders, coaches and parents with a practical resource to improve performance quickly.

Goaltending is a complex position in a complex sport. In the end, like anything, it can be over-complicated to a point where performance is compromised. Here, we have established ten essential improvements that can be made to your game without excessive intervention or teaching required.

Leo and I have labored hard to condense our thoughts into these 10 (plus honorable mentions) meaningful improvements. As technical coaches, it is difficult to walk away from so many technical improvements that can be made to your game, however, the word "Quickest" always came back to us as we compiled the list. Additionally, we had to consider the many inputs into an athlete's performance. Some inputs are mental while others are athletic and still others are equipment or technique based. This handbook does not focus on a single category. Instead, we have compiled the quickest and most tangible self-help methods of improving your game and stopping more pucks regardless of source. To be certain, they are all straightforward and they will all meaningfully improve your game.

Like anything in goaltender development, repetition, discipline and self-initiative are the keys to success. The improvements noted here, for the most part, require these three self-driven attributes. The improvements are not complex. They simply require your attention on a full-time basis.

If you are disciplined, these things will become instinctive and habitual. They take little in the way of additional physical effort. Therefore, if you can accept the notion of "full-timing" these concepts, we can assure you that your game will improve and improve quickly. Falling into the "part-time" trap will limit the power of these concepts.

As you embark on this read, do not under estimate the power of our Honorable Mention list. While they have not made the "10" list, they have dramatic affects on performance as well. You should consider these a part of your broader list and all of these should form a part of your philosophical approach to the position and your performance.

Roberto Luongo illustrates exceptional positioning fundamentals and reactive capabilities in making this save.

#**1**

GET MOBILE

Movement and mobility is the cornerstone of your technical game. The beauty of this first improvement is that it is simple and it can be totally self-directed – it just needs your commitment.

Hockey is a dynamic sport that demands that the goaltender have great efficiency around the crease. This allows you to match the pace of the play and puck movement. Additionally, as a goalie, your movement ability lies at the foundation of nearly every play. Here's an example.

As the play develops, the goalie establishes initial position. This positioning is achieved using movement skills. As the play continues to unfold, the goalie makes adjustments to this position. Yes, that would be your movement that is refining this position. Notice that your entire positional game is fueled by these movement skills. We know that positioning is vital to our game. Therefore, the engine that fuels our positioning must, in fact, be more important since it must come first. Let's consider this further.

Statement 1

If my movement improves then by default my positioning should improve. This makes good sense. As I become more controlled on my skate blades and become quicker from point A to point B shouldn't I be able to hit a greater number of my positional targets? The answer is yes. So, it is true that as my movement efficiency progresses, my positioning has no choice but to follow in a positive way.

Statement 2

If my positioning has improved (because my movement improved) wouldn't it be fair to claim that, on average, my first save would be made with greater control and, therefore, also on average, be more successful. Certainly, if I am out of position and out of control then my first save can't be under control and, if I am out of position, my save percentage most surely is on the decline. If we can agree to all of this then it would be safe to extend our argument by saying that improved movement leads to improved positioning which leads to improved first-save success.

Statement 3

We can go further. If my first-save has become more controlled and has a greater success rate then shouldn't my rebound control be better. Clearly, rebound control is not a consideration when I am struggling to make the save. If, however, I am under control, well positioned and the save is straight forward then it would be reasonable that I would be better able to manipulate the rebound. Additionally, a well-controlled save is also directly related to more dynamic recovery.

We can see then that a mobility/movement improvement will result

With the puck coming across Luongo's slot, he loads his push skate properly and tracks the puck laterally across the net. His mobility and movement skills allow him to combine great size and positioning in support of his game.

in an across-the-board improvement in my fundamental game. This fundamental game is best defined as my positional/save execution/ recovery abilities. There is no other skill gain that can have this kind of overwhelming and all-encompassing impact.

To enable you to make these gains, we have assembled the twelve best movement patterns that will, with diligent and disciplined work, deliver this type of improvement to your game. You'll note that you only need to do four of these patterns each practice for the allotted repetitions and keep cycling through the twelve patterns. You will complete the twelve every three practices.

Familiarize yourself with the legend to the right so that you understand the symbols associated with each movement pattern.

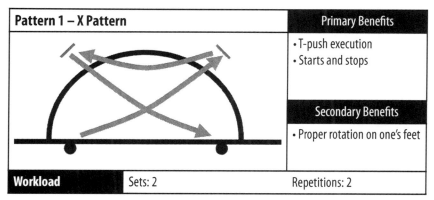

LEGEND			
SYMBOLS/MARKINGS		ABBREVIATIONS	
T-push		Butterfly	BT
Shuffle (from feet)		VH Position	VH
Backside Push (from BT)		Narrow Butterfly	NB
Knee Shuffle (from BT)		Distance Carry	DC
Butterfly Slide (from feet)		Quick Trigger	QT
Set Point			
Depth Gain			
Momentum Build			

Pattern 1 – X Pattern	**Primary Benefits**
	• T-push execution • Starts and stops
	Secondary Benefits
	• Proper rotation on one's feet
Workload	Sets: 2	Repetitions: 2

Clark's Development Comment:
This is a simple and common drill used by goalies of all ages to improve one's T-push, edge control and rotation on one's feet. Stop and set at each point to ensure proper development of your starts and stops and expedite development of your edge control.

Luongo's Quick Tip:
Always lead with your eyes. This is a simple and important issue because as you move from Point A to Point B, you get an early read as you move to your new target. Reads are truly the key to the great netminders' games.

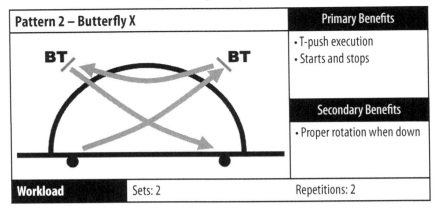

Pattern 2 – Butterfly X	Primary Benefits
	• T-push execution • Starts and stops
	Secondary Benefits
	• Proper rotation when down
Workload — Sets: 2	Repetitions: 2

Clark's Development Comment:

This, too, is a simple and common drill used by goalies of all ages to improve one's T-push, edge control and, in this case, rotation on one's knees. Development of good rotation will improve one's "angle" game which is the positional key to modern goaltending.

Luongo's Quick Tip:

Rotation, when down, should involve the planting of the backside foot so that this edge can push you directly to your new target. Many goalies fail to rotate properly which results in a wrong path moving from Point A to Point B.

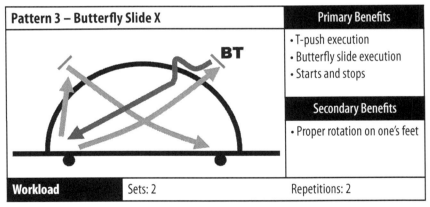

Pattern 3 – Butterfly Slide X	Primary Benefits
	• T-push execution • Butterfly slide execution • Starts and stops
	Secondary Benefits
	• Proper rotation on one's feet
Workload — Sets: 2	Repetitions: 2

Clark's Development Comment:

This is a continuation of our X series of drills which now combines not only T-pushes and rotation but also butterfly-slide work. This is important because the butterfly slide is a primary lateral move that transitions a goalie between their "up" game and their "down" game.

Luongo's Quick Tip:

When doing a butterfly slide it is important to drop or collapse the lead knee close to the ice before pushing. An early push without this drop results in a loss of power which, in turn, means you may come up short of your new angle.

Pattern 4 – Backside Push X

Primary Benefits
• T-push execution
• Backside push execution
• Starts and stops

Secondary Benefits
• Proper rotation when up
• Proper rotation when down

Workload	Sets: 2	Repetitions: 2

Clark's Development Comment:
This is the final X pattern in our series and introduces a goaltender to the backside push. This is another primary lateral move that allows a goaltender to cover wide lateral distance while staying down throughout.

Luongo's Quick Tip:
When executing a backside push there is two keys for me. First and foremost, you need to play with sharp skates. In order to push my body across the ice, I need a sharp edge to anchor this move. The second thing is to lift the lead knee slightly off the ice. This will load your back skate further securing your push.

Pattern 5 – Perimeter

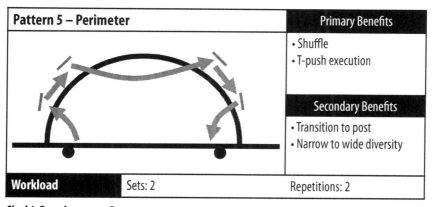

Primary Benefits
• Shuffle
• T-push execution

Secondary Benefits
• Transition to post
• Narrow to wide diversity

Workload	Sets: 2	Repetitions: 2

Clark's Development Comment:
A goaltender must develop all facets of their lateral game. This includes the T-push, butterfly slide, backside push, shuffle and knee shuffle. In this drill, we combine the narrower shuffle with the wider T-push. A combination of these moves helps a goaltender track perimeter puck movement in their zone.

Luongo's Quick Tip:
We call this the Perimeter Pattern because I use it to work on the flexion in my stance. I don't like to get too low and too wide early in the attack. When the puck is moving around the perimeter, I try to have only partial flexion. This makes me quicker and more mobile leading into my shot preparation.

Pattern 6 – Reverse Perimeter	Primary Benefits
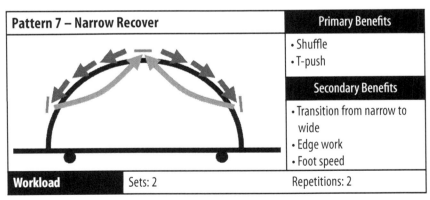	• Shuffle • T-push execution
	Secondary Benefits
	• Depth maintenance • Transition to post
Workload Sets: 2	Repetitions: 2

Clark's Development Comment:
Due to the importance of in-zone tracking, we have added a second perimeter pattern. This pattern helps not only build strong crease movement but also helps establish, instictively, a goalie's middle depth.

Luongo's Quick Tip:
My middle depth is "heals out" so when I do these patterns, I always try to drive out to this depth and maintain it above the crease. Of course, when I transition to the posts, I am giving up depth as I approach this point. In other words, off the bad angles, I am deeper so that my transition to the post is easy and smooth.

Pattern 7 – Narrow Recover	Primary Benefits
	• Shuffle • T-push
	Secondary Benefits
	• Transition from narrow to wide • Edge work • Foot speed
Workload Sets: 2	Repetitions: 2

Clark's Development Comment:
A second pattern that focuses on a blend of narrow and wide movements. This is the nature of goaltending. Since we don't get to control the play, we have to be prepared to mix up our movements by changing the width of each move and also having a rapid change in direction to track unpredictable puck movement.

Luongo's Quick Tip:
It is really important to develop great edge control and foot coordination. As goalies, we operate in small spaces so our ability to shift direction and have rapid starts and stops is really important to our positional success.

Pattern 9 – Post Transition

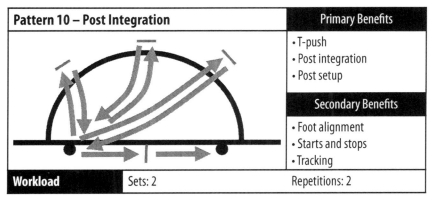

Primary Benefits
• Forward adjustment
• Combining shuffle and depth management (backward shuffling)
• Transition to post

Secondary Benefits
• Tracking
• Positional range

Workload	Sets: 2	Repetitions: 2

Clark's Development Comment:
One of the most difficult moves for a goaltender, in actual game play, is the transition to the post. It is the one moment in the game where a goaltender must remain set and prepared for a save despite having to go off square with their feet, shoulders and hips. A smooth transition to the post, through relentless pattern work like this, will reduce "sloppy" goals.

Luongo's Quick Tip:
Patterns, like this one, have become part of my movement regime because they bring control to an awkward part of the game. The point of transition is tough for all goalies so working in this area, while awkward, makes great sense.

Pattern 10 – Post Integration

Primary Benefits
• T-push
• Post integration
• Post setup

Secondary Benefits
• Foot alignment
• Starts and stops
• Tracking

Workload	Sets: 2	Repetitions: 2

Clark's Development Comment:
As a continuance of post integration, this pattern highlights a very important net-play concept. It does not matter how you arrive at your post, you want to have the same basic alignment "upon" arrival. The word "upon" is the key. As you arrive, you want to have proper alignment NOT after you arrive. This pattern helps build strong integration but also develops "upon arrival" positioning on your post. This will quickly eliminate sloppy goals around your net.

Luongo's Quick Tip:
Post play is a challenging part of the position because of post interference. Having regimented patterns, like this, helps to make post play smoother and helps the body become more accustomed to post play. The really important part of this pattern, though, is ensuring good foot alignment. This allows me to quickly adjust to handle a back-door feed or a play to the nearside.

Pattern 11 – Narrow Up Rotation

Workload	Sets: 2	Repetitions: 2

Primary Benefits
- Forward adjustment
- Shuffle
- Narrow adjustment

Secondary Benefits
- Rotation when up
- Depth maintenance
- Angle maintenance

Clark's Development Comment:
Movement efficiency throughout your positional range is essential. This pattern combines a host of movement skills. A very useful aspect of this pattern is the combination of large moves with small moves. This mimics actual game play. Too often patterns do not reflect the realities of the game.

Luongo's Quick Tip:
Working small moves is really important to my game. Since my legs are long, I am at risk of pushing past my angle. Using patterns like this helps me keep my positions accurate.

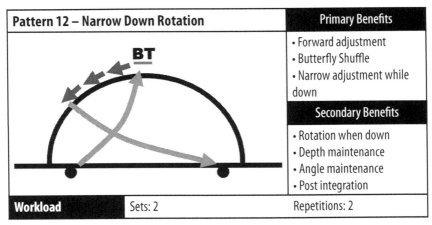

Pattern 12 – Narrow Down Rotation

Workload	Sets: 2	Repetitions: 2

Primary Benefits
- Forward adjustment
- Butterfly Shuffle
- Narrow adjustment while down

Secondary Benefits
- Rotation when down
- Depth maintenance
- Angle maintenance
- Post integration

Clark's Development Comment:
This pattern is similar to our previous pattern with the only difference being the small moves are down while in the butterfly. This adds another important combination to your movement work – long moves, short moves, up moves and down moves all combined into a single pattern. Again, the emphasis is to not only cover the full gamut of moves but combine them in realistic sets.

Luongo's Quick Tip:
As a butterfly goalie, I use the butterfly shuffle just like I shuffle on my feet. By adding this skill to the patterns allows me to not only be efficient on my feet but also on my knees. This set of patterns covers the full spectrum of movements and will, over time, improve your entire game.

SAMPLE SEASONAL WORK PLAN

In this seasonal plan example, we are cycling through the twelve patterns every three practices.

	Practice 1	Practice 2	Practice 3
Pattern 1	X	Perimeter	Post Integration
Pattern 2	Butterfly X	Reverse Perimeter	Post Trasition
Pattern 3	Butterfly Slide X	Narrow Recover	Narrow Up Rotation
Pattern 4	Backside Push X	Rush Cross Ice	Narrow Down Rotation

When you feel that you have mastered these patterns, visit the GDI website (gdihockey.com) and get Phase 2 patterns. You can also visit us here to see these patterns executed in HD video so that you can check on your progress. Here's a tip. Have someone video tape you doing these patterns then login to GDI and compare your executions with those on the GDI website. When you feel like your movements are similar to the GDI video, you can graduate to the Phase 2 patterns.

Please note if you see the GDI logo adjacent to any of these patterns, you can see these patterns on GDI's Youtube channel.

#2

UNDERSTAND AND HONOR THE SAVE PROCESS

One of the most effective ways to improve your game, which requires zero skill but immense discipline is the honoring of the save process.

Every save involves three key components:

1. Preparation

2. Save execution

3. Recovery

In practice, most goalies only focus on the save execution. At first glance, this seems to be the most important aspect of the save process. However, it is really the least important from a process standpoint. Goalies that have poor preparation, inevitably, have inconsistent performance and, at best, average results.

The great goalies of the game understand the pivotal importance of their preparation. In fact, preparation, for a goalie, is similar to an assist on a goal. Most goals never occur without an assist. Likewise, most saves require the ASSISTance of strong preparation.

Preparation includes the initial positioning, adjustments off this initial position, ice awareness, presentation, setting and other attributes. All of these things are obviously important and lead to more effective save execution.

Recovery falls on the opposite side of the save execution. When we really think about this aspect of the save, it becomes clear that recovery is nothing other than preparation for the next shot. Therefore, it can be stated that almost everything a goaltender does is prepare. Think of a game in which you face 25 shots. In that game, the actual time it took you to make the 25 save executions was probably 25 seconds. In your sixty-minute game, then, preparation activity accounts for 59:35 of the total.

Luongo tracks the puck carefully with his eyes which allows him to seamlessly move to his next position. The save process involves not just the save but the preparation prior to the save and the recovery after the save. Honoring this full sequence in practice ensures expedited development.

Now, to further consider the importance of honoring the save process, think about the following:

In an average practice, a goaltender might have 200 shots. Imagine the volume of good repetitions that are available to the goalie that prepares effectively.

- ~75 t-pushes
- ~350 shuffles
- ~200+ rotations
- ~200+ stops

- ~200+ starts
- ~150 visual trackings
- ~50 backside pushes
- ~50 knee shuffles
- ~200 head swivels for awareness purposes

The goalie that does not adhere to the save process loses all of this developmental opportunity. The goalie that commits to the save process, developmentally, might look like the dark grey line in Chart A. On the other hand, the goalie that fails to honor the process would look more like the light grey line in this chart. This is NO exaggeration. In fact, we have probably credited the "dishonoring" goaltender with too much development in this chart.

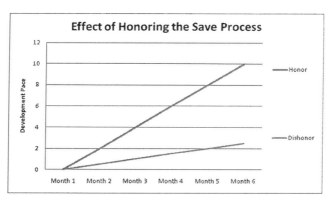

As we can see, by recognizing the importance of this approach the "honoring" goalie has an exponentially quicker development pace.

Technical development in any position, of any sport, is based upon repeatedly executing sound mechanics. The greater the volume of quality repetitions, the quicker the skills are mastered. One cannot underestimate the power of this process.

This brings us to an important concept that must be raised at this stage. This is the quality of one's work. The following mathematical examples highlight the importance of quality repetitions. When we combine volume and quality, we find the combination that generates the fastest developmental pace.

	Goalie A	Goalie B	Goalie C	Goalie D	Goalie E
Good	2	4	6	8	10
Poor	8	6	4	2	0
NDR*	-6	-2	+2	+6	+10

*NDR - Net Development Result

We illustrate five goaltenders each executing 10 repetitions of a given skill. We have rated them on the number of good repetitions and the number of bad repetitions. This is important because many athletes fail to recognize that you don't just get credit for the good repetitions. Poor repetitions are detrimental to development because each bad rep has an equally counteracting effect on the good repetition. Therefore, it is very important that you minimize the poor repetitions in order to maximize one's Net Development Result (NDR). You can see in the following chart the results of poor quality executions. Don't miss this self-development opportunity.

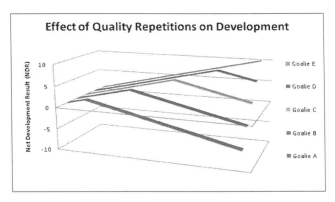

We can see that the Goalie A, due to poor quality, has had a significant developmental decline. Meanwhile, Goalie E, who has executed each repetition with high quality, has an extraordinary NDR.

When we combine the honoring of the save process with exceptional practice quality, we achieve the goalie's fastest development track.

With this information now in mind, get to work in practice. Development pace is in your hands.

#3

DEVELOP A PUCK-COLLECTION HABIT

The purpose of this handbook is to provide goaltenders and coaches with ten meaningful ways to improve a goalie's game significantly and quickly. This particular habit may, actually, have the most immediate and direct impact on game success. By definition, we are talking about the action of collecting or gathering loose pucks after a save.

The habit of collecting loose pucks is a simple but powerful skill that will reduce the number of goals against. Roberto Luongo never fails to collect a loose puck in practice which ensures that this instinctive ability is razor-sharp in a game.

The reason that most goalies do not collect ALL available pucks is because it seems trivial. One of the greatest goalies ever to play the game, Roberto Luongo, is a testament to the non-triviality of collecting the puck. There is never a puck which is within gathering distance that he does not draw into his possession. Interestingly, there are few goaltenders that have the rebound control that he does. Much of his puck control comes from this collection habit.

There are many options when it comes to a loose puck:

1. Ignore it
2. Sweep it away
3. Follow it but don't collect it
4. Collect it sometimes but not others
5. Collect it always

Let's examine the pros and cons of each option.

IGNORE IT –When the goalie simply chooses to ignore it there are a host of problems. Most significant is that it was impossible for the goalie to be visually attached to the puck through the save process. They are training their muscle memory to NOT refill space when these pucks are at the side. The development opportunity to improve the speed and coordination of gathering in these pucks is lost. The ability to cover a loose puck is delayed due to the ignorance applied to the process. Finally, and most critically, in all of the negative cases is the fact that ONLY when the puck is in the goalie's possession can the goalie feel confident that the puck will not end up in the back of the net. This goalie is simply ignoring this benefit. Actually this isn't a benefit, it is the goalie's basic responsibility – to stop pucks and prevent them from ending up in the back of their net.

SWEEP IT AWAY – In the second case, the goalie chooses the opposite action as the desired habit. Instead of collecting and gathering in, the goalie is choosing, as a matter of habit, to sweep it or push it away and back into the play. First off, this is a habit in and of itself. This formed habit will transcend itself into the game. While the goalie may be moving the puck out of the current danger spot, there is no guarantee that it isn't ending up in another, or even worse, danger spot. The puck remains in play. Not only does the goalie not know who might get possession of the loose puck but also does not, ultimately, know if the puck will end up in the back of their net – 2, 5, 10 or 15 seconds later.

FOLLOW IT BUT DON'T COLLECT IT – In the third case, the goalie follows the loose puck when it is off to one side or the other but does not actually draw it in and possess it. While the goalie is following the puck with both eyes and body, which is very important, there is a lost opportunity to retain and control the puck. Furthermore, the coordination that can be established by gathering pucks that have come off the body or pads is lost.

COLLECT IT...SOMETIMES – The final negative approach is the part-time approach. Part timing any activity does not establish habit. Habits are instinctive actions that have been created through tireless repetitions. If you choose to cover the puck once but not the next time then you have zero growth. Once again, as we mentioned in Chapter 2, you do not get to take a "plus" for a good execution without taking a "negative" for a bad execution. Therefore, the part-timer who does everything kind of fifty/fifty never makes progress because they are always losing the benefit of their previous good repetition.

Yes, this improvement is trivial.

Its trivialness, however, is not in its importance but rather in how much effort it takes. The volume of effort required to gather a loose puck is the only thing trivial. Trivial by definition is small and inconsequential. Well, collecting a loose puck, from the perspective of effort, is trivial because the effort required is so tiny and so inconsequential to one's total effort that to not adopt this habit is nothing short of mind boggling.

The goaltender plays the key role. The goaltender plays a leadership role. The goaltender has the single largest, individual impact on team success. To adopt these "trivial" habits is not an option for the responsible goaltender. This goalie recognizes their role and seeks out competitive advantages. As described at the beginning – this one is a big one!

As a concluding note, we would like you to think about the following. For the vast majority of your game, you react to everything going on. In other words, you are the recipient of the play. Everything funnels down to you and you respond to whatever hand you are dealt.

When you have an opportunity to control the game – seize it! This is why you want to develop a great puck-collection habit. When you control the puck everybody reacts to you because you are controlling the game.

#**4**

BUILD TWO ANCHORS

Highs and lows are part of the game and, more succinctly, part of the position. The great goalies find ways to extend the highs and minimize the lows. One of the most important things that one needs to do is recognize the danger of "over compensating". This is very common for athletes. Athletes that care want to find solutions when their performance suffers. They try harder. They focus more. They prepare with greater intensity. These are examples but to be clear over compensating can be as dangerous as under compensating. A common adjective for "under compensating" is, simply, lazy.

It's hard to imagine that "trying harder" and "focusing harder" can be put in the same category as being lazy but the effects can, indeed, be the same. For certain, if continued poor performance or even worsening performance is the result of both then there's a parallel.

One of the very best ways to extend the highs and minimize the lows is to build two critical anchors into your game, which are derived from the three main elements of positioning:

1. Angle
2. Depth
3. Body

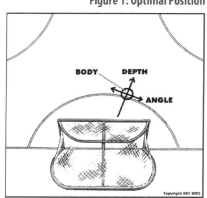

Figure 1: Optimal Position

These are the three ingredients that go into a goalie's position (see Figure 1 - on previous page) and it is here that we find a goalie's two anchors.

We know, or we ought to know, that angle is a goalie's positional priority. In fact, angle is the only thing that a goalie possesses that provides net coverage in and of itself. Think about this for a moment. Take the butterfly. If a goalie is in a butterfly but behind the net, it doesn't provide any net coverage. Let's take depth, if you are one hundred feet from the goal line but at the side boards, you have no net coverage. These may be ridiculous examples but they illustrate the point. Everything that you do must be associated with an angle or it has no coverage value.

Middle depth is a vital anchor in your game. Understanding your depth game helps maintain the consistency and stability of your performance.

Remarkably, angle is NOT one of the two anchors and the reason is simple. A goalie's angle is not flexible. It is a geometric fact. Goalies don't go off angle when they try harder. Instead, they come out further. They get deeper into their stance. So, a goalie's anchors lie in the two flexible aspects of positioning – depth and body.

Let's define the word "anchors" as used in our context. These are tangible things within our game that are flexible and they tend to be the items that are subconsciously adjusted in order to find solutions. A better approach to consistent and high performance goaltending is to intimately know exactly where these anchors need to be so that they are not over compensated causing further problems. Since they are "anchors", the knowledge of where they are calms the goalie's game during troubled times and provides a base "to come home to" from which confidence can be drawn.

THE DEPTH ANCHOR

Positional Range

CONSERVATIVE

AGGRESSIVE

Middle Depth

The depth anchor ensures that a goalies depth does not damage their game. In our depth spectrum, you can see that the two ends are conservative and aggressive. The first anchor is one's middle depth. Middle depth is defined as the depth the goalie commonly plays at. For instance, the following middle depths are common:

- Top of the crease

- Heals out

- Toes in

A good indication of middle depth is the typical depth that the goalie WANTS to play at during in-zone play. In-zone play is a good indicator because the goalie does not need to manage speed (e.g. against the rush) so middle depth is the common depth positioning during this game dynamic. We say "want" because a goalie's depth can easily get corrupted. As a goalie's game tanks, goalies want to try harder and might feel they need to get more aggressive. This doesn't work so they try to be more conservative and as this pendulum swing begins, the goalie's game strays further and further from "home" despite good intentions.

The second aspect of the depth anchor is positional range. If a goalie knows their middle depth then their positional range surrounds this spot. The goalie's positional range is used to help manage the speed of the rush. If a goalie's middle depth is top of the crease, for example, then their positional range would be approximately two feet above and eighteen inches below. Combining middle depth and positional range we have defined the goalie's depth game and the goalie, knowing this personal definition, will not over or under compensate with depth. The goalie knows that their best performance occurs when their depth is managed within this range. This is vital to performance consistency and limiting the downward spirals in the goalie's game.

THE STANCE/BODY ANCHOR

Like depth, stance also can be adjusted and is, therefore, an anchor. As goalies "try harder", they get lower in their stance. As they lower the stance, the feet get wider. As both of these variables are affected, the goalie's mobility diminishes. Here's an example whereby the under compensator may actually have an advantage compared to the over compensator. A taller, narrower stance (which is easier to maintain from an energy standpoint) provides more mobility than a lower, wider stance. The issue, once again, is to define your stance anchor within your personal approach.

Like depth, stance flexion is another important stabilizing anchor in your game. Understanding your basic flexion helps you avoid over compensation when things aren't right. Combining knowledge of "your" depth and flexion will allow you to reduce the low points in your season.

You have two primary stances:

1. Basic, mobile stance

2. Save stance

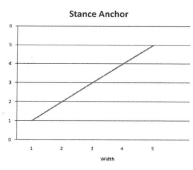

Stance Anchor

Your basic, mobile stance is the one that we are concerned about when we are discussing your stance anchor because it is the stance that you prepare in. The save stance is that final stance that you settle into right before the save and it is, indeed, lower and wider than your basic stance. However, if your basic stance gets corrupted then you will not be able to optimize position (most specifically angle) on the puck.

Figure 2

Figure 3

A goalie wants to define both stance variables for their basic, mobile stance. These two variables are flexion and width (shown in the graph above). Flexion is the degree of bend in the knees and hips (see Figure 2) and width is the width of the skates (see Figure 3). A great marker for stance width is skate width relative to shoulder width. This can help a goalie define their width. For example, one might determine that "my basic stance width is slightly outside shoulder width". A very good goalie example of this width marker is Roberto Luongo of the Vancouver Canucks.

Flexion is a little tougher to mark so it will require more creativity. Here's an example of a marker. "When I am in my basic, mobile stance my knee and hip flexion allows the toe of my stick to touch the ice when tilted". A very good goalie example of this specific flexion marker is Marc-Andre

Fleury of the Pittsburgh Penguins.

Anchors are essential to maintaining effective performance. Building these two anchors will allow you to underscore your game with consistency, logic and a quick remedy when troubled storms strike.

#**5**

DEVELOP A PRE-GAME ROUTINE

Great performance is spawned from a familiar place. It is not a random event but is germinated from past actions. Many sport psychologists and other mental-skills coaches will have you go back and recall your great performances. They do this because they want to check in on your mental frame of mind and physical state that was present at that time. They want to know about your mindset heading into that performance. They want to know how you felt during that performance. They try to take a snapshot of your state and for good reason. You didn't on that day become a better physical goaltender. Your technical skills and athletic acumen from the week prior to that performance didn't suddenly change. A host of other more intangible elements collided that brought that performance to pass.

These elements might have included:

- You underwent a certain set of preparational activities
- Your meal sat well inside you due to the type of food and the timing of intake
- You had a good rest (either the night before or that day or both)
- You had a really good practice a couple of days earlier
- Your body was limber and warm
- You had a relaxed but focused warm-up
- You took control of the game early by talking and communicating with your teammates
- You were well hydrated but not bloated and bogged down

- Your gear was fresh and dry
- Your skates were sharp and honed

Of course, this is a random set of ideas that we have compiled. The reality is that there was a convergence of things, events and activities that brought you to a place that then allowed you to have that mind-numbing performance. Remember, you didn't become a better or worse technical or athletic goalie over night. Only your mind and your preparation can change you that quick and, therefore, you need to take great care of obvious preparational activities that allow your body to perform optimally. You also need to bring your mindset into that common and familiar place that supports "your" elite performance.

All told, this is your routine.

Routines are fantastic sequences of activities that bring you "home". Your "home" is that spot within yourself where your game and performance feel most comfortable and secure. Many goalies have very rudimentary routines. Indeed for many young goalies their routine begins when Mom or Dad yells up the stairs – "OK, Johnny, it is time to go!" Your game, and the position of goalie that you have obligated yourself to, demands more than that. You are the captain of your team. That's right. You play the most crucial role and, therefore, by default, you have the greatest preparational obligation. Flippancy and trivialness are unacceptable approaches.

The development of a pre-game routine is vital for all goaltenders. It brings the body and mind into a unifying place where your optimal performance will stem. As your career evolves so too will your pre-game routine. The important thing to do is, like Luongo, have one.

The following short routine-building exercise will help you get started. Remember that every person's routine is unique. The hope of this handbook and this exercise is that it plants the seed of a routine. You begin testing things out and soon your routine will begin to take hold. The important point is that if you want consistent, high-level performance a routine is a MUST.

BUILD A ROUTINE

Use the following subheadings and subsequent spaces to frame your routine. If you already have one then mark it down. If not, use this as your template. Remember that a routine is a routine. It occurs in the same fashion and the same order every single time. We need to bring our mind "home" where optimum performance is found.

#	Detailed Description	Duration
MY PRE-GAME ROUTINE		
	Rest Plan	
e.g.	Bed at 10:00 pm the night before	N/A
1		
2		
3		
	Nutritional Plan	
e.g.	Pre-game meal 4 hours before game time (spaghetti, salad and OJ)	N/A
1		
2		
3		
	Music/Video/Mental Preparation Activity	
e.g.	Play my pre-game playlist on the way to the rink	20 min.
1		
2		
3		
4		
5		

Physical Warm Up		
e.g.	1 hour before game lateral calisthenics	7 min.
1		
2		
3		
Locker Room Sequence		
e.g.	Lay out gear in specific fashion before starting lateral calisthenics	1 min.
1		
2		
3		

#6

ROTATE BEFORE YOU ACTIVATE

Of the ten improvements in this handbook, this is really the only technical element. There are some broad technical concepts like "be more mobile" but as for true mechanical improvements, this is the only one.

What does that tell us? Well, it tells us that there is an awful lot that goes into great goaltending. It also shows us that while goaltending is a unique endeavor that greatness in the position shares similarities with greatness in any endeavor. Great athletes prepare effectively. Great athletes strive for improved athleticism. Great athletes are respectful of their game and the demands and habits required driving their game to the desired level. The essence of this is that the fundamentals of greatness are universal to all endeavors.

With this said, the mechanical side of the story is another element. Like the technical precision of the world's great gymnasts – mechanics fit into the formula of success. Before we delve into the notion of "rotate before you activate", let it be said that mechanical excellence comes only with superb discipline and attention to detail.

This section of the handbook offers us the opportunity to focus a little on practice habits. While we want to provide ten simple ways to improve your game, these opportunities to harp on key traits cannot be passed up.

Since angle is the most important thing to Luongo's positional game, his ability to rotate plays an equally important role. It is rotation that fuels strong angle play. Here Roberto begins to rotate his torso in preparation for a full rotation and recovery to the puck's new position.

We want you to examine the graph to the right.

As you can see in our graph, the goalie with superb attention to detail has a much steeper development advance when compared to the goalie that trivializes

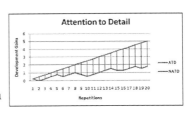

the quality of their mechanical work. To be certain, technical ability is an input into success. Goaltending is a potpourri of skills. Technique is a part of this mix and, therefore, must be honored on the ice. The no-attention-to-detail (NATD) goalie is flippant. This goalie does a nice job a couple of times in a row but is then tired so does some poor repetitions. They catch their breath or get mad because a couple of goals go in so they "straighten up" but then someone hits them in the mask with a high shot and they get off again. This kind of erratic technical behavior will destine you to a painfully slow development pace.

Now, back to the main improvement concept of this chapter – rotate before you activate. We will use a series of diagrams to illustrate the notion of rotation but the following line diagrams will help us begin to understand.

You'll recall from earlier discussion that angle is our positional priority. You'll further recall that angle is the only asset that a goalie has that covers net in and of itself and, additionally, that all of a goalie's assets only have coverage value if they are attached to strong angle positioning.

This is the key to this improvement – rotate before you activate. Proper rotation is the engine behind a goaltender's angle positioning during dynamic game activity. We say "dynamic" because your initial angle, as the puck approaches your zone, may come from simply stepping away from your goal line. Once the play is upon you, however, the dynamic aspect of hockey is upon you and this is where rotation is vital to your angle game.

In Figure 1, we see three line drawings. These drawings, collectively, represent the notion of rotation. Take a moment to read the instructional caption at the bottom of the drawings. You'll notice that in Fig. 1A the goalie did not rotate as evidenced by the thick black arrow. This goalie would need to take an arc out and around the top of the crease to propel them, eventually, into the new angle shown by the light grey triangle. One can easily see that not only is this a long distance but, more importantly, during the goalie's travel from Point A to Point B they remain outside the light grey triangle for the majority of the distance. This means they have **NO** net coverage.

In Fig. 1B, we can see that the

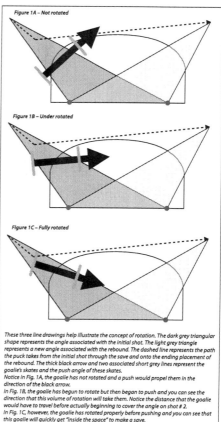

Figure 1A – Not rotated

Figure 1B – Under rotated

Figure 1C – Fully rotated

These three line drawings help illustrate the concept of rotation. The dark grey triangular shape represents the angle associated with the initial shot. The light grey triangle represents a new angle associated with the rebound. The dashed line represents the path the puck takes from the initial shot through the save and onto the ending placement of the rebound. The thick black arrow and two associated short grey lines represent the goalie's skates and the push angle of these skates.
Notice in Fig. 1A, the goalie has not rotated and a push would propel them in the direction of the black arrow.
In Fig. 1B, the goalie has begun to rotate but then began to push and you can see the direction that this volume of rotation will take them. Notice the distance that the goalie would have to travel before actually beginning to cover the angle on shot # 2.
In Fig. 1C, however, the goalie has rotated properly before pushing and you can see that this goalie will quickly get "inside the space" to make a save.

goalie has partially rotated. In this case, the goalie is much better off as evidenced by the direction of the dark arrow. This goalie will get into the light grey triangle faster and have a greater likelihood of making the next save. The fact, however, remains that the majority of this goalie's positional adjustment lies outside of the light grey triangle. As we know from Fig. 1A, when we are outside of this triangle, we have **NO** net coverage.

Finally, we have the goalie in Fig. 1C. This goalie has fully and properly rotated. Remember, a goalie's assets do not have value unless they are associated with an angle. This goalie, due to proper rotation, will enter the light grey triangle the fastest and, therefore, will have the greatest likelihood of stopping the subsequent shot.

This is a strong representation of rotation. Now, let's make sure we understand the actual improvement we are seeking – rotate before you activate. We know what rotate means but what is "activate". This is the weighting of the push skate. Once you apply weight onto the push skate, your rotation will cease and this will lock the push angle of your movement. Therefore, we must rotate before we activate (or weight the push skate).

Figure 2 highlights the activation of the backside foot.

Connecting the importance of strong attention to detail to your rotation mechanic is very important to your development and can, indeed, be a rapid and near immediate improvement to your game. The caveat is that you must attack this improvement with superb attention to detail in your practice executions.

#7

COMMUNICATE!!!

Talk about an easy and dramatic improvement to your game. A team is effective as an operational unit, not as a set of independent and unconnected parts. Stated another way, the old cliché that "the whole is greater than the sum of its parts" is exactly what we are talking about.

While goalies are largely confined to a small area of the ice, it does not mean that they cannot

WHEN IT COMES TO COMMUNICATING WITH ONE'S OWN DEFENSEMEN, HODGINS FEELS THAT SUBTLETY IS NOT A VIRTUE.

contribute to the team unit. Naturally, the goalie's responsibility is to stop pucks and that contribution to the team unit is the foremost contribution that can be made. Of course, it is great if you can get out of your net to stop rims, make a few passes and help out transitionally where possible. However, without question, the simplest contribution that a goalie can make is to talk.

The goaltender is, in effect, a spectator for the vast majority of the game. Think about a 25-shot performance by a goalie. At the same time, let's presume three additional things:

1. Each shot is engulfed by 20 seconds of intensive preparation and post-save activity

2. For every shot that reaches the net there is an additional shot that requires the same amount of intense activity but these shots don't make it to the net

3. The game is 45 minutes in length

All told this goalie has a total of 2,700 seconds of playing time. Within this time, the goalie is intensely active for 50 total shot attempts at 20 seconds each. This equals 1,000 seconds in which the goalie is pre-occupied with intense puck-stopping activities that precludes them from making any other contribution to the team. This means that for 1,700 seconds, the goaltender is watching the game. That equals 63% of the game.

Since you need to be on high alert all the time, you are conscious of all of the game's nuances. You see it all. Your teammates on the bench do not. Your coach does not. You are the only person in the building that is fully in tune with what is taking place on a full-time basis.

For instance:

- Your coach is offering feedback to the players that just got off the ice.
- Your teammates that just changed are grabbing a drink of water and catching their breath.
- Your parents just went for a bucket of popcorn.

So, you, the goalie, are the only one that is intently watching every second develop.

That's right; you ought to be the only full-time communicator associated with your team. You see it all. You need to take it upon yourself to relay important information to your troops. You are the compass and you are the radar for your team.

Master the following commands as a minimum. As your confidence improves you will find that you will, within the context of your team's specific systems, increase the number of commands, the succinctness of your commands and the volume of your commands. There is no better place, as always, to improve this aspect of your game than practice. Don't be bashful…don't be scared. This is your responsibility.

Basic communication glossary and protocol

Command	Meaning
BACK DOOR	Tells a defender to be aware of a back-door or weak-side threat
FAR-SIDE SUPPORT	Tells a retreating teammate that support lies on the far side
FREEZE IT or EAT IT	Tells a teammate to take a whistle
ICE IT	Tells a teammate to get a break by intentionally icing the puck
MAN ON	Tells a retreating teammate that there is severe pressure
NEAR-SIDE SUPPORT	Tells a transitioning teammate that support is available on the near-side boards
PARTNER	Tells a defender to use his partner as an outlet
REVERSE	Tells the transitioning teammate to reverse the direction of the puck to eliminate the first forecheck
SCREEN	Tells a teammate that they are screening the goalie
SET IT UP	Tells a teammate to slow things down, typically behind the net, and to set up a controlled break-out (often used on the power play)
SLOT	Notifies a teammate that there is an uncovered slot presence
SLOW IT DOWN	Tells the teammate to slow things down so that the squad can re-collect themselves
TIME	Tells a teammate that there is limited to non-existent pressure
TURN IT UP	Tells a teammate to immediately pivot with the puck and head up ice
USE THE CLOCK	Tells a teammate not to rush and to strip time off the clock. This is typically done late in a game when the team has the lead
WHEEL or GO	Tells a teammate to accelerate with the puck in the existing direction. Players associate this command with the availability of time

Now remember when you begin to talk on the ice, in support of your teammates, use these four fundamentals:

1. **SHORT COMMANDS** – Short commands are easier to understand

2. **ARTICULATE** – Say them articulately – go ahead and say the word **A R T I C U L A T E L Y** – your teammates need to understand what you say

3. **LOUD** – There's lots of ambient noise in the building – you must be LOUD and CLEAR!!!

4. **UNDERSTAND TEAM SYSTEMS** – You can't yell things that don't support the systems that your teammates have been taught to play or commands they don't understand

#8

GET MORE FLEXIBLE

Hockey is a dynamic and unpredictable sport. Despite the very best intentions, goaltenders cannot always predict and cannot always train their mechanics to meet every need. There are those moments in a game that unfold exactly as they are supposed to. For instance, a player drives down the wing, the defender closes the gap and a shot is taken off the wing. There is no deflection, there is no screen and the goaltender cradles the puck simply on the chest. Indeed, the majority of attacks follow a somewhat predictable pattern. The goalie needs to subconsciously select from their wide arsenal of trained skills the appropriate response to each of these patterned moments. These plays, however, do not define the great netminders.

It is the unpredictable, dynamic moments of the game where great goalies stand up and are counted. Therefore, you need to assemble a set of skills that supports not only the patterned side of goaltending but the unpatterned side. Arguably, the most important skill to support these unpredictable moments is flexibility. The reason for this is simple. Hockey is a game of limited time and space. This is particularly true of action around the crease. Without time, a goalie cannot muster a mechanical response and, therefore, an athletic response is often the only possible action. Goalies need visual acuity, agility and flexibility to fight these battles. It is important to note that flexibility is a precursor to agility. You cannot be exceptionally agile without flexibility and range of motion.

So not only does flexibility allow you to be more agile and athletic, in a general sense, but it also serves two additional puck-stopping purposes:

1. Split-second saves
2. Forward saves as opposed to backward saves

SPLIT-SECOND SAVES

As described, hockey is a sport of limited time and space, for all players. For the goalie, not only can puck movement, player to player, be quick and tough to keep up with but the puck also can career off of skates, shin pads and sticks. This makes it impossible to track the puck's angle constantly. There are moments when you just can't keep up to the pace. If one of these moments is a scoring-chance moment then the goaltender will be forced to cover space not through adjusted position but by stretching and reaching.

The flexible goaltender has a dramatic advantage in these split-second moments. The goalie that can reach an additional six inches due to their rapid extension, fueled solely by their flexibility, will pick up additional key saves – the saves that define the great goalies.

Flexibility is the most important element associated with making instinctive, difficult saves. The reason for this is that most of these saves occur due to lack of time. Therefore, the ability to stretch into them is the only way that the save can be made with this time constraint. Luongo's athleticism allows his already long limbs to reach those extra inches to steal goals from opposition sticks.

FORWARD SAVES VERSUS BACKWARD SAVES

Another important reason for outstanding flexibility relates to the notion of coverage and position. The inflexible goaltender, as they begin to extend, reaches the outer limit of their range of motion. The muscles stop but the play continues. Without exception, inflexible goalies will fall backwards so that they can reach backwards to try to keep up with the play and remain competitive. This creates all kinds of issues, most notably:

1. Holes and gaps in coverage
2. Falling back and away from the puck exposes the vertical angle
3. Perpendicular faces of a goalie's gear are lost

These exposures are illustrated in Figures 2A and 2B.

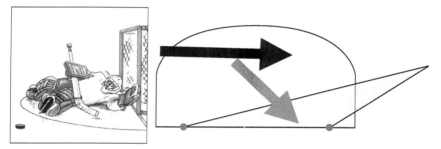

The "forward" goalie, which demands excellent flexibility, eliminates these deficiencies. In addition, this goalie enjoys the benefit of more logical and fool-proof net coverage in these desperate/dynamic moments. Goalies should cover the net from the bottom up. In other words, cover the ice and then progressively build vertical coverage from the sealed ice upwards using the perpendicular pad face with hands and arms stacking the coverage vertically.

You'll note in Figure 3A and 3B (next page) the differences in coverage between the "backward" goalie and the "forward" goalie. Again, it is flexibility that drives this "forward" approach.

 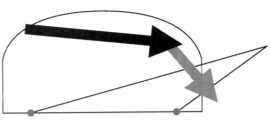

To conclude, the beauty of flexibility is that it is 100% in your control. This isn't an intangible. This improvement is as tangible as it gets. If you claim to have the ultimate desire to be the best then this stone cannot be left unturned.

There are thousands of well-trained goalies in the world. Why? Goaltending, in general, has improved which has had a trickle-down effect through our natural desire to mimic. More importantly, goalie coaching and its quality and availability have spread throughout the hockey world. Therefore, to be good mechanically, in essence, only makes you average in today's competitive goaltending marketplace.

Seize the flexibility advantage to drive your game another notch up on the competition.

SUGGESTED FLEXIBILITY RESOURCES

1. **RELAX INTO STRETCH** by Pavel Tsatsouline
2. **STRETCHING** by Anderson

Both of these books are available online.

You should consult with an exercise physiologist before embarking on any significant training activity.

#9

UNDERSTAND YOUR RELEASE POINT

Goals are scored predominantly in four ways:

1. Traffic complications
2. Net play
3. Rush attacks
4. Rebounds

If we were to assess all of the goals scored in hockey, the vast majority of goals would fall into these four categories. Goaltenders often work on traffic. Goaltenders often work on their net play. Goaltenders often work on rebound control. Unfortunately, goaltenders get very little tutelage on rush attacks.

The reason is simple – goalie coaches are often given small spaces to work. They are given an end zone or below the circles or just around the crease. Also, more sophisticated coaches use boutique-sized rinks. The bottom line is that rarely does a goaltending coach have the opportunity to work rush chances in a repetitive manner. Sure there are plenty of team drills that are done during practice but the goalie coach doesn't get to intervene and correct much. These "flow" drills keep going and the goalie coach is left to watch and wait until the end of the drill to offer any guidance. By this time, the team has moved onto another drill and another focus while the coach is left scrambling to get his "rush" correction across.

With all of this said, the ability to manage the rush is really a testament to a goalie's ability to manage their depth. This is the one time in the game when you have to manage speed. Unlike in-zone plays which are more static and lateral for a goalkeeper, the rush demands that the goalie manage their depth in unison with angle, squareness and body positioning. These added complications test a goalie's timing, positioning and overall command of their game.

Most goalies, like Luongo, await the attack from their goal line. It is from this point that a goalie will step out to face the attack once the puck crosses their release point. In Roberto's case, the far blue line represents his release when facing the rush.

When Luongo releases, he gets out to the top of his positional range so that he can face the rush with an effective and versatile position. Managing the rush is difficult due to the speed of the rush. Roberto manages it by moving out past his middle depth so that he has some depth to give back as the rush progresses closer.

One of the most important elements of rush management is a goalie's release point. Defined, the release point is the goalie's timing when they pull away from the goal line. In game terms, it is when the play is in the opposite end, the rush begins and the goalie steps out to face the rush. There are a couple of lines of thought here.

1. **Release late to improve your angle** – a lot of goalies release late because this gives them an accurate angle when the attack is more developed. In other words, if the goalie steps out as the play hits center ice or their own blue line, the attack will be closer to fruition and the goalie's initial angle will be more accurate.

2. **Release early to help manage depth** – a more sophisticated, but simple, approach is to release earlier. A good reference point would be to step out to one's depth as the play comes across the far blue line. While this is earlier in the attack and it may not yet be fully developed, it gives the goaltender a much better opportunity to manage their depth.

Figure 1 – Release Point Overview

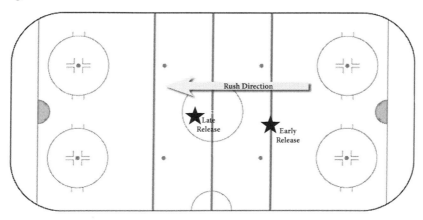

Depth is a "game killer" or a "game supporter". In our discussion around building anchors we referenced this and we will reinforce this here. Consider the following additional benefits of an earlier release point:

- **Positional Range** – an early release allows a goalie to use their full positional range which is one of the fundamental skills associated with rush management [Figure 2 – Positional Range]

- **Forward Momentum** – an early release allows the goalie to get stable at their "rush depth" rather than scrambling out late or, perhaps, never achieving it due to a late release

- **Timing and Pace** – an early release allows the goalie to dictate their timing and pace – remember rush management is really speed management which can only be handled with depth adjustments – a late release forces the goalie to get out and back too quickly OR to not get out enough and get caught flat footed unable to manage the speed of attack

- **Team Transition** – an early release provides the goalie with easy and direct access to the back boards to handle the dump in – a late release forces the goalie to "hairpin" around their net to get to the boards [Figure 3 – Angle to Backboards]

Figure 2 – Positional Range

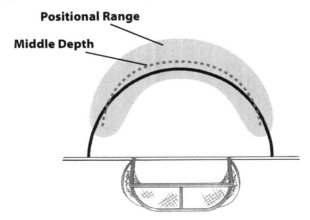

A goalie's positional range is really a "rush" concept. Since much of a goalie's in-zone activity is lateral, middle depth is the primary distance used. Off the rush, however, the goalie must manage speed and, therefore, the goalie's positional range comes into play. The basic concept is that the goalie will release out to the top of their positional range and use this additional depth to help manage the speed of the attack.

Figure 3 - Transition Angle to Boards

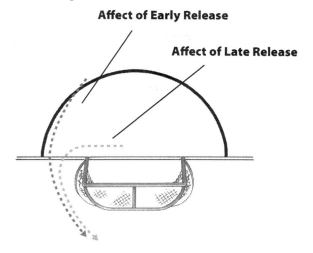

Affect of Early Release

Affect of Late Release

An early release allows the goaltender to access the back boards more directly. As seen here, the released goalie can take a direct path to the back boards allowing them to get there quicker and with greater control. The late release goalie needs to "hairpin" around the net.

Without question, an early release provides you with a more comprehensive set of benefits then a late release.

As a concluding point, it is important to manage your position with the additional depth associated with your positional range. You do this through shuffling but giving up depth with your shuffle. This ensures that angle and squareness are in place as the speed of the rush pushes you backwards into the middle of your positional range. Figure 4 highlights this type of "backward" shuffling. You'll notice that on each lateral move there is a drift backwards. This brings us to another important concept which is your "transition point". This is defined as the point in the rush when you will quickly transition to a post position. You'll note that the "release point" occurs at the beginning of the rush and the "transition point" occurs at the end of the rush. The "backward" shuffling helps bring you closer to the post position in order to simplify your transition to the post.

Figure 4 – "Backward" Shuffling

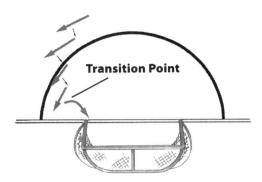

"Backward" Shuffling

Transition Point

Backward shuffling is the method of lateral adjustment that allows you to not only stay on angle and square to the rush attacker but also gives up the additional depth that was established at the beginning. The ability to manage the speed of the rush while maintaining angle and squareness illustrates the goalie's command of their game.

Arguably, the rush is the goalie's most challenging game situation. The adept goaltender that gets this side of their game under control is that much closer to conquering their game and establishing themselves as an elite netminder.

For additional information on rush management visit gdihockey.com.

#10

BE AWARE

While we could have put down as our number one most important improvement "read-and-react skills", this is a journey of untold proportions. Therefore, it didn't meet our criteria for "quickest" improvements. With that said read-and-react skills can not only be improved through experience but through some simple improvements. There are a handful of basic fundamentals that will lead to improved anticipation and reads. General awareness is one of these basics.

Awareness of the ice is crucial at all times. It not only allows you to identify pressure and support when handling the puck (as Luongo does here) but it also improves read and anticipation skills as well as your communication ability. Always seek to have your head on a swivel during games and practices to help develop this awareness advantage.

So, rather than overwhelming you with a complete read-and-react analysis, our focus is to help you set the stage for improved anticipatory skills.

Figure 1 - Ice Awareness

Here's the read-and-react or anticipatory framework for a goaltender:

1. Early awareness of the attack and its specific nuances

2. Read of puck-carrier intent

3. Continued peripheral awareness

4. Final read of puck-carrier intent

5. Visual tracking through the save process

6. Start again with #1 and repeat read framework

As you can see the first step in one's read framework is awareness. The simple ability to keep your head on a swivel early in the attack provides enormous information to the "reading" goaltender. If you think about reading a play this all makes sense. You'll note the second item in the read framework – "Read of puck-carrier intent". Clearly, a strong understanding of the attack and the various options associated with it provide essential support to reading the puck-carrier intent.

For example, if a three-on-two breaks up the ice, the tunnel-vision goalie, who lacks awareness, focuses solely on the puck carrier. At no point, as the rush develops, does the goaltender consider the back-door player driving the far post. This means that the most likely plays that the puck carrier can make include shooting off the wing or driving the net. When the puck carrier does something that is counter to these options, the tunnel-vision goalie is surprised and confused and ends up caught flat footed. The aware

Figure 2 - Timing of Awareness

goaltender, on the other hand, that has monitored the full attack, through awareness, is not surprised by the puck-carrier's actions but rather these actions feed directly into their anticipatory skills and a correct judgment can be made.

The process and timing of ice awareness are fairly straight forward. As the attack unfolds, you want to do a quick survey of the attack. In other words, quickly identify what format the attack is. If it is a rush, is it an "odd" attack or is it an "even" attack. If the play is in zone, is there a weak-side attacker or does the defensive posture have good position. These are all things that occur in a goalie's early awareness of the situation. Then, the goalie wants to shift to a stronger focus on the puck carrier. Excessive focus on weak-side attackers is not helpful because the true dictator of the play is the puck carrier and that is where the most important read is made. However, it is awareness that makes your read of puck-carrier intent make sense. In other words, awareness gives your read validity and you can be more confident in committing to this read.

Once the early awareness has been established and you are familiar with the oncoming attack, you focus on the puck carrier. However, your peripheral vision will continue to provide an "awareness" benefit. Since you understand the main attack dynamics, your peripheral awareness can continue to help monitor and confirm things. In the end, however, the puck carrier always dictates the final execution and, thus, the importance of puck-carrier intent.

All told, awareness is the precursor to read-and-react skills. The great thing about becoming more aware is that it not only helps you begin to build your read-and-react game but, in doing so, it is totally unobtrusive to your game. Very few skills carry this last attribute. The reason that awareness is so unobtrusive is that it is done early in the attack when the play is not dangerous. It is simply a habit you need to establish. As the puck comes out of the opposite end, simply demand of yourself that you have a quick visual survey of the ice.

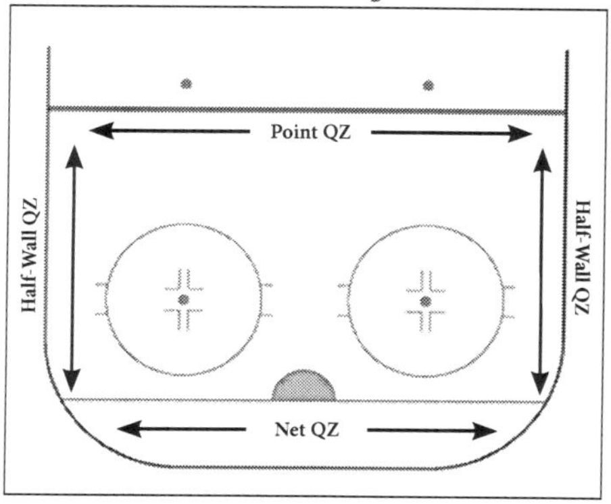

For in-zone play, it is also simple

Figure 3 - Quiet Zones

because we use "quiet zones" to establish our awareness timing. If the puck is in a quiet zone then the goalie can survey the ice. So, you ask, what is a quiet zone? A quiet zone is defined as an area of the defensive zone in which the goalie is not at risk of a shot. The most obvious areas of the ice that are representative of this quiet-zone effect are the outsides. Use Figure 3 (previous page) as an illustrative example of quiet zones. Notice they reside exclusively on the perimeter.

So, develop a simple awareness habit to not only provide an immediate improvement to your game but to also begin to establish vital read-and-react abilities.

HONORABLE MENTION

We have identified our 10 Quickest Ways to Improve Your Game but we would be remiss to not mention these five additional essential tips and strategies. These additional five items carry significant weight. Indeed, it would be easy to suggest that this handbook should be characterized as the 15 Quickest Ways to Improve Your Game. So, don't forget these gems:

1. **Play with sharp skates** – This might be the easiest and most overlooked item. Your edges propel you from position to position. Skate edges that fail at a key moment can be the difference between a save and a goal. Proper equipment maintenance, in general, and, specifically, with your skates simply stops more pucks.

2. **Early eyes** – This is the second simple and unobtrusive fundamental associated with your read-and-react game. You'll recall that we introduced to you the importance of "awareness" in our top-10 listing. "Early eyes" is the next fundamental that will open up your read-and-react game. The main emphasis here is that when the puck moves from one spot to the next, the goalie must lead their positional adjustment with their eyes. Having "early eyes" on the puck enhances your ability to read the shooter's intent.

3. <u>**Don't over invest in the first shot**</u> – You are not a better or worse goaltender based upon the first shot of the game. In fact, you are the very same goaltender. So, don't get caught up emotionally in this first shot. Sometimes the other team can make a great play right off the opening draw. This doesn't mean you are destined to a poor performance. It means that the opposition made a good play. This needs to be parked immediately so as to not do further damage to your performance and your team's chance for success.

4. <u>**Work in practice/Play in games**</u> – That's right – your practices are for work and thought. Your games are where you get to enjoy the fruition of your work. Games are why we work. We get to enjoy the fruits of our labor in the game. So, the moral of this improvement is do not over-stress yourself in games – this is the fun stuff so enjoy it!!!

5. <u>**Battle to the finish**</u> – In practice, you must battle and compete for every loose puck. Being a part-time competitor makes you a non-competitor. When a puck is loose, you don't stop. Your job is to prevent pucks from crossing the goal line. Under no circumstances can this responsibility be taken for granted or be given token emphasis. In practice, develop your personal rule that, after warm-up, "no pucks cross the goal line". Furthermore, if a puck is going to beat you, the shooting player will have to go way beyond the call of duty to score that goal. You will not back down… In time, this will make you better, your teammates better and get into the heads of the opposition.

CONCLUSION

We have provided you with 10 quick ways to improve your game. However, the very best tip that we can give you is right here. YOU need to take responsibility for your game and your improvement. Remember the following mantra and these improvements will take hold and your development and performance will take off:

You are your best goalie coach

When you embrace this mindset, your potential is truly unlimited because you have taken responsibility for your growth, development and performance. Goaltending coaches, like us, can help facilitate improvements in your game and can be partners in your growth but nobody can have the impact necessary that you yourself warrant.

So, take these 10 improvements and the five honorable-mentioned items and get after your game. Watching goaltenders like Roberto, Marty, Marc-Andre and Cam work on their game you will see their level of commitment, attention to detail and, above all, the responsibility they take for their own growth as the ultimate keys for their success.

Waiting for others to develop your game is a sure-fire way to mediocrity. Ian Clark cannot be the catalyst. Leo Luongo cannot be the catalyst. As mentioned, we can be there and we can facilitate but we cannot direct your future success – only you can author that story.

Stay tuned for additional handbooks in our "10" series.

Good luck in your goaltending and we wish you the very best as you challenge your game to the next level.

Ian Clark   Leo Luongo

ADDITIONAL RESOURCES

For comprehensive information on all aspects of goaltender development use the following two essential online resources:

gdihockey.com – GDI, the world leader in goaltender training, has a comprehensive online learning suite. The following online applications are designed to improve your game:

- **Online Coach** – This function allows members to search and view technical "lesson plans" on all aspects of goaltending. Information provided includes both textual and graphical information.

- **TRENDkeeper**™ – GDI's proprietary performance analyzer evaluates a goaltender's game using 24 distinct variables. TRENDkeeper™ provides printable reports, developmental action plans and drills geared towards the development of personal weaknesses and desired improvements.

- **Drill Database** – This follows a similar process as our Online Coach. Members can peruse drills following a logical navigational/search process. Drills are presented with a graphic, key development points and complete drill description.

- **Online Clinics** – This function provides a series of seasonal online clinics. These multi-media events offer detailed content using text, illustrations, photos and videos to enhance the learning experience. Additionally, the system uses workbooks and quizzes to help facilitate development and understanding

- **STATkeeper**™ – This tool allows a member to track all key statistical elements within their game including:

  - Record

  - GAA

  - Save Percentage

  - Shutouts

  - GPR™– Goalie Power Rating™ - this is GDI's proprietary statistical ranking that calculates a goalie's winning efficiency, shutout efficiency, inverse opposition scoring efficiency and inverse scoring/game ratio and compiles it into a single number (the GPR™ is modeled after the NFL Quarterback Rating System and places a peak-performing goaltender in and around 100 on its scale)

BIOGRAPHIES

IAN CLARK

 Ian Clark has been a NHL Goaltending Coach since 2001 when he joined the Florida Panthers. In July, 2002, he joined the Vancouver Canucks as Goaltending Consultant and has remained with the organization ever since. A former resident of Vancouver, Clark currently resides in Dallas, Texas and is the Founder of GDI-The Goaltender Development Institute. He was also the Editor-in-Chief of "From the Crease" and "The Goalie News", leading development publications for goaltenders of all ages and skill levels.

Clark has been a member of Team Canada's World Junior Championship coaching staff for four years and helped lead the team to two consecutive gold medals in 2005 and 2006. Recognized as one of the leading educators of the goaltending position, Clark's knowledge and innovative training has attracted high-performance goaltenders at the NHL, minor pro, major junior and NCAA levels.

Clark has worked with many of today's leading netminders including Roberto Luongo, Cam Ward, Marty Turco and Marc-Andre Fleury to name a few. Clark-trained goaltenders can be found in 21 of 30 NHL organizations.

LEO LUONGO

Leo joined GDI as a Regional Manager in 2007. He has studied under goaltending instructors François Allaire and GDI Founder Ian Clark, as well as his brother, NHL goaltender Roberto Luongo. Currently, Leo is a Goaltending Coach/Consultant in Montreal where, for more than four years, he has successfully developed goaltenders of all ages. He has provided instruction at many summer camps alongside François, Roberto and, separately, Ian Clark.

As a goaltender, Leo played elite level hockey his entire career. He is currently the goalie coach for the Acadie Bathurst Titans in the QMJHL and is considered one of the top up-and-coming goalie coaches in the game.

The 10 Secrets to Great Rebound Control

The next in The 10 Series of handbooks on goaltending is *The 10 Secrets to Great Rebound Control*. One of the lost arts of the goaltending position has come back into focus. Through the 90's and 00's goaltending went through a technical transformation that, in many ways, detracted from quality rebound control.

Strict focus on movement, positioning and the power of butterfly goaltending created an army of "drop and block" goalies who learned to cover space. This diminished reactivity, in favor of blocking, and hampered a goalie's ability to control pucks.

As goaltending shifts into a new phase, goalies are learning to build upon the strengths of this recent generation while recapturing the lost arts of the position – one of which is superb rebound control.

Learn *The 10 Secrets to Great Rebound Control* in the next handbook by NHL Goaltending Coach Ian Clark and up-and-coming goaltending coach Fabio Luongo. From control on the body to the stick to the blocker and, most importantly, the pads, Clark and Luongo break down the methods that will allow you to stop and control more pucks.

NOTES

Made in the USA
Lexington, KY
11 April 2012